Emotional Intelligence at Work

A Self-Help Guide That Teaches You to Build Your Social Skills and Establish Strong Relationships with Your Peers

By Lawrence Franz

Table of Contents

Introduction 3

Chapter One: Improving Interpersonal Connections at Work 5

Chapter Two: Controlling Emotions 18

Chapter Three: Building Confidence and Finding Long-Lasting Success 32

Chapter Four: Social Engineering and Leadership 45

Conclusion 59

Introduction

Thank you for downloading *Emotional Intelligence.* Workplace stress is one of the worst health problems plaguing the modern world, accounting for 12.5 million work days lost in the United States alone as of 2016. Workplace stress also causes many physical and mental health problems. Among these are migraines, heightened blood pressure and heart rate, chronic anxiety, and paranoia, to name a few. Within the following chapters, we will go over some of the more useful methods of handling emotions within the workplace, and day to-day life as well.

There are many facets of emotional intelligence that are extremely useful in the workplace that are often ignored. All too many people take new jobs, gain bad relationships with their coworkers, do not try to resolve their issues, and flee promptly. This hardly works in the short term and never works in the long term. If tools to handle emotions are never gained, then the same issues are always going to arise despite the workplace or living situation. If you have problems with working, then why not solve the problem at its source—your emotions?

This book will feature advice on a number of topics: improving interpersonal connections at work, controlling emotions, building confidence, finding long-lasting success, social engineering, and leadership. In all of these subjects, the reader should find at least one thing to take away from all this. Emotional intelligence is not something which should be underestimated. It can be one of the most important traits that a person can have or develop throughout life.

There are many great books on the market covering this subject. Thank you again for downloading this one. Enjoy!

Chapter One:

Improving Interpersonal Connections at Work

A workplace can often be a demanding, high-stress environment to find oneself in. All this pressure can be amplified even higher when interpersonal connections are either not being made or are in bad conditions in the workplace. This is why it is of the utmost importance to improve the relationships one has with their coworkers and to keep improving on them continually. In this chapter, we will look at some useful tips and techniques for improving relationships with coworkers and working more effectively within group settings.

The first step in improving relationships with coworkers would have to be a check on your own workplace stressors. Before trying to fix what is going on with other workers, it is important to try to fix whatever is going on with you. To manage stress from the outward would be to hit the bullseye on the wrong target. Some of the most common workplace stressors that plague most modern employees are excessive workloads, low salaries, work that is not challenging or engaging, lack of opportunity for enhancement or growth, lack of social support, unclear performance expectations or conflicting demands, and lack of control over job-related decisions. Odds are that, if you are employed, one or more of these stressors apply to you. There is no shame in this, in fact, it is the norm, with around 65% of Americans citing their top source of stress as being work.

This epidemic of workplace stress is especially problematic because of its effects on the health and well-being of workers. Short-term stress is one thing, causing stomach aches, headaches, sleep disturbances, difficulty concentrating, and short temper. It is long-term stress, however, that causes the more dire effects, such as insomnia, anxiety, high blood pressure, and immune system weakening. This is where stress becomes very dangerous and potentially deadly. Most do not deal with their stress until it becomes a problem, but once it does, it may already be too late. This is why it is important to apply skills in coping with workplace stress.

One way of coping with workplace stress is to keep

track of your stressors throughout the day. This can be done easily through journaling your inner thoughts throughout the day. Another way is to respond to stress in healthy ways. Rather than coping with unhealthy comfort foods, alcohol, or tobacco, you could try exercising, practicing one of your hobbies, or trying something new whenever you start to feel stressed out. Taking periods of rest is another important one that many neglect to do in these times, but effective working is just not possible without an occasional break. To work constantly is to build up a house on foundations of sand. Meditation is also crucial. This is like a reset for your brain, which will not only reduce stress but improve focus when working on individual tasks. And finally, it is always beneficial to receive support. Speaking with a friend, family member, therapist, or coworker can always take a lot of pressure off.

Now that some means of dealing with stress in the workplace have been discussed, we can get to improving relationships with coworkers.

The role of coworkers in the average American's normal life has changed dramatically throughout recent years. A coworker used to be a much more formal acquaintance to the average worker. Today, however, many spend more time with their coworkers than they do with their friends and family. The search for more meaningful work has many things that come with it, among these is the added emphasis on having a strong team behind your back and the desire to be a strong team member. Neither of these two is possible when getting along with your coworkers becomes difficult. Having good relationships with your coworkers is also important in career development. Getting better job opportunities can, like most things, often come down to winning a popularity contest.

There are many different means of securing good relationships that differ widely with time and circumstance. A few will be listed below:

Keep it simple

When starting at a new company, it can often be beneficial to meet with all your new coworkers one by one and informally. First impressions speak volumes, so taking an initiative in greeting others can help you in the relationships you establish in the long run. This process can also make the orientation process a lot easier for the more shy among us.

Humility and gratitude

People do not typically appreciate working with arrogant people, or people who aren't open to criticism. These attitudes will make it much harder to make friends, and people will generally try to avoid working with others who project these ugly traits. It is always important that you let your coworkers know that you are open and receptive to criticism and new ideas and it is also important that you avoid stepping on their toes with an arrogant attitude. Thanking people for their work and helping them along the way will also make people more agreeable to you.

Listen and observe actively

In the average workplace, as in anywhere else, it is usually a good idea to gain an understanding of the culture that surrounds you and its norms before criticising it. If you want to keep a good standing with your coworkers and bosses, it is important to show respect for the company and those who work for it. This will not only help you but others around you when they invariably try to emulate your performance, creating a better overall work environment.

Transparency and honesty

It is impossible to work with others without conflict. Not only is avoiding this conflict unsustainable, but it also hinders development. What is always more important is that you are able to deal with conflict productively and maturely whenever it arises. Under these circumstances, it becomes important to take responsibility and to avoid carrying blame too far. You should also never neglect to apologize when it is necessary.

Keep a clear expectation of the work relationship

Goals are usually more easily reached when sought after with planning to an end in mind. You do not have to turn communication with coworkers into some type of Machiavellian mind game, but you should be precise in what you say to others and keep preformed goals in mind when speaking with coworkers at times. This tip is especially useful for managers and bosses. Give the people below you a clear example of what the company wants from them and try to make your demands accessible yet practical. The more clarity that is provided to workers, the more confidence those workers will typically have when meeting the demands placed on them. Workers at all levels should avoid ambiguity when discussing work-related issues with others. It is important to remain objective and practical when discussing these matters, and any other attitude will generally be met with confusion and frustration.

Encourage and engage

Employees work best on a diet of praise and recognition about every two weeks. It is normal to desire being seen through your work and for your work to be acknowledged. It is not just a weightless platitude to assert that praise and recognition carry further among employees than do salaries and benefits, it is the truth. As Maya Angelou said, "people will forget what you said, people will forget what you did, but people will never forget how you made them feel." If you make people feel inferior, lazy, or useless, they are going to remember that you did that. If you make them feel valued, competent, and important, they are likewise going to remember that you did that.

Remember that coworkers are only humans

The expectations that you should place on your coworkers should always be grounded in reality, and erring on the side of minimalism. You only have the right to expect from coworkers about as much as you have to offer, whether that be a lot or a little. Try to always remember that your coworkers, whoever they might be, are just as human as you are. With that being said, it becomes important to come to know the people working around you. You should try to come to know what interests, hobbies, personal lives, dreams, and aspirations they have. Allow them their privacy, but show them that you take a personal interest in their happenings. The more that you do this, the stronger bonds and relationships you will develop. Getting to know who works around you can make not only your work life but also your own inner life all the more meaningful.

Embrace differences between individuals

It is easy to underestimate the difficulty in getting to know new coworkers. It can be very intimidating or even frustrating to go through this process, especially with coworkers who can be disagreeable or tyrannical. These are normal issues to confront though, and ones that never go away. Knowing how to deal with these people and situations can be tricky, as there are no manuals or textbooks that teach how to, but erring on the side of professional courtesy is a must. Seeing the people you work with more as humans and less as coworkers is always beneficial in supporting strong relationships. As humans, those who you work with are bound to differ from you in a wide variety of ways. Always be respectful of those differences, as they are usually good things for you to be around. Also, in modernity, it is important to remain cognizant of your own conduct at every moment of a workday.

Develop your people skills

As you already know, good relationships start with good people skills. These are otherwise known as "soft skills." Some examples of soft skills that are advantageous to have in the workforce are leadership skills, proclivity toward teamwork, problem-solving skills, communication skills, flexibility/adaptability, work ethic, and interpersonal skills. All of these skills have one common theme: sociability. Without being sociable with your coworkers, you can never expect to build and maintain good relationships with them, nor can you expect to build and maintain your career. If you are not sociable, then you may remain at the bottom of every work hierarchy that you find yourself in, or you may not even be able to keep work.

Identify your relationship needs

This one is closely related to the one on keeping a clear expectation of the work relationship, but it is also important to be clear with yourself and others about what you need to work properly. It is not fair to let yourself get bullied into relationships and situations that do not work in your favor. You have a right and an obligation to serve your own best interest, and this can be done effectively without making other people around you suffer. The first step in doing this, however, is specifying your needs. This is most easily done by journaling on what bothers you and brainstorming methods of fixing the issues at hand. Once skills in doing this are developed, they can be applied to any and all facets of your life, it just takes the initiative to get this ball rolling.

Schedule times to build relationships

Scheduling a time period is one of the best things that you can do for yourself in the contemporary world. This is also true for building relationships. Even if the time each day is minuscule, 5 to 20 minutes, for example, over time this practice can and will help to improve the relationships with your coworkers.

Appreciate your coworkers

If there is one thing that everyone who you ever work with is always going to want, it is an appreciation for the work that they do. If you keep in mind that everyone else is doing more or less as much as you are doing then appreciating them becomes much easier. Showing that you are thankful for the work that others have to offer will invariably open the door to better relationships and even boosted company morale.

Positivity is important

Focusing on remaining positive will not only help you with your mood and well-being, but it will also help those around you. Positivity is a trait that is attractive and contagious, and it makes working (and living) much easier and enjoyable. Negativity, on the other hand, is repellent and leads only to further suffering. Remaining positive not only improves your relationships with your coworkers, but it also boasts many health benefits, including lowered heart rate and blood pressure, a strengthened immune system, lower levels of cortisol and blood clotting, less muscle strain and heartburn, lower levels of chronic pain and disease, and even a longer average lifespan. With all things considered, a person really can't even afford negativity.

Controlling and managing boundaries

Managing boundaries becomes important when there are uneven distributions of time and energy being spent on the people and things that you work with. For example, if one coworker of yours wants to speak with you for hours out of every day while another never speaks to you, it could be a good idea to close that gap. While working, it is never a pleasant feeling to be spread thin. Meanwhile, it is ill-advised to neglect to keep enough on your plate. To maintain balance boundaries sometimes need to be set. It is important to be assertive while doing this also. If you cannot afford certain social interactions, then there is no shame in turning them down politely.

Gossip is a destructive force

The biggest killer of workplace companionship is usually gossip. This is also the most cowardly means of getting your points across, and it should be avoided at all costs. When an issue with a coworker arises, it is always important to address it directly with the coworker in question and usually no one else. Playing office politics often ends badly for all parties involved and seldom gets any problems solved.

Active listening

When a person speaks, they want reassurance that they are going to be listened to. If they are not listened to, then there is no reason why they should speak and, just like that, a coworker becomes ostracized and alienated. This is why it is important to listen actively to what a coworker says and to absorb the contents with an open mind. If you do this, people will be more inclined to trust you, and you will become more admired at your place of work.

Improving workplace relationships can be one of the most difficult aspects of keeping a job but, if done effectively, it can make working much easier and more enjoyable. It can be pretty surprising to see just how quickly things in a workplace can plunge into chaos if these steps, or others like them, are never taken by anyone. Once plans for improving relationships are administered within a workplace, however, the whole of the company improves, yourself included.

Chapter Two:

Controlling Emotions

The workplace can be one of the most difficult places to control emotions in. No matter how hard you try, those difficult days are always bound to come up. In your personal life, your reactions to stressful situations are much more free, but in the workplace, your reactions are subject to the scrutiny of your coworkers. Any emotional outbursts while working can not only damage your professional reputation and productivity, but they can even get you fired.

Under normal circumstances, it is usually easy to maintain composure in the workplace, but under more stressful circumstances, such as staff layoffs, budget cuts, and department changes, staying calm can prove difficult, if not impossible. Under these circumstances, however, it becomes even more important to keep your temper, as bosses typically consider the demeanor of their employees when deciding who gets laid off. You have complete freedom on how you react to certain situations, but that freedom comes with responsibility, especially in the workplace.

It may seem easy to decide how you're going to react in certain situations with hindsight, but it is always advisable to explore techniques in dealing with these situations and emotions. Here, we will discuss many negative emotions associated with employment, as well as many methods of coping with these emotions.

The most commonly reported negative emotions among workers are as follows:

Worry/nervousness, frustration/irritation, dislike, anger/aggravation, disappointment/unhappiness

And now we will get into some strategies in dealing with these unhealthy emotions.

Worry/nervousness

These are two of the most unpleasant and unhealthy emotions on the spectrum, and, unfortunately for workers, these two emotions plague virtually every workplace. This anxiety can stem from a number of sources: fear of getting laid off, social problems, low salaries, large workload, and so on, and be compounded with problems at home, or with family or friends. A small amount of stress can be a productive thing, but once it becomes chronic anxiety, health problems start to occur. Here are some tips on how to avoid excessive anxiety:

Break cycles of worry

Do not surround yourself with anxiety. If you can foresee needless anxiety stemming from a situation or a conversation, avoid that anxiety. Try to minimize the number of anxiety inducing things that you have to deal with.

Try deep breathing exercises

These help primarily to slow down your breathing and heart rate. There are all sorts of different deep breathing exercises that you can learn about on the internet. For one, there is cyclical breathing, breathe for 4 seconds followed by holding for 4 seconds, and then out breaths for 4 seconds followed by holding for 4 seconds. When doing these exercises, it is important to focus on your breathing and nothing else. In addition to these exercises, there are other physical relaxation exercises that will help reduce workplace stress, including progressive muscle relaxation.

Focus on improving the situation

Whatever it is worrying you in regards to work, brainstorming solutions and making attempts at them will help reduce your anxiety. Doing these things will also make you a more valuable asset to your company.

Journal your worries down

Simply writing down the things that bother you will do a lot to alleviate the anxiety surrounding them. This technique also helps to curtail sleep problems and nightmares, as worries that we write down during the day don't typically bother us by night. Once these are written down, you can then schedule times to deal with these issues. Before that time comes, let these issues leave you and go about your day. When that time comes, make sure to perform a proper risk analysis before putting any plans into place.

Worry and nervousness can decrease self-confidence and lead to health complications. it is always important to trail these negative emotions away and remain confident and secure.

Frustration/irritation

Frustration is more often than not caused by the feeling of being trapped or stuck at a point that you want to get out of, but cannot. This feeling can be caused by a number of things, especially at work. A colleague blocking a project of yours, a boss too disorganized to catch a meeting on time, or a phone call held out longer than necessary are just a few examples that come to mind. Frustration, whatever its causes, should always be dealt with quickly because when it is not, it can accumulate into anger and other even more negative emotions.

There are, however, many ways of dealing with this awful emotion, a few of which are listed below:

Stopping to evaluate

The best thing to do when feelings of frustration arise is to stop what you are doing and take the time to evaluate them. Writing your frustrations down in this stage can help. After this is done, think of some positive aspects of your current situation. This will improve your mood and reduce further frustration.

Look for positive things

Again, finding silver linings in a frustrating situation will make you see the events unfolding in a new light. This change in your thinking will improve your mood, among other things. If it is a person who is causing you frustration, then keep in mind that it is probably not personal, and if it is an event or situation, then it can probably be solved. Try to move on from this step as much as possible.

Recall the last time you felt frustrated

If you can remember the last thing that you were frustrated about, then you can probably remember how that thing eventually resolved itself. Looking at things with hindsight, they always work out fine. You can also probably recall that your feelings of frustration did not do much to help you in that last situation, so to assume that they are helping you this time around would not be very prudent. Perspective is everything, and so many issues lose so much of their stature when seen from different angles.

Dislike

Dislike for certain coworkers is inevitable, and when it pops up, it seldom goes away. We all have to work with people who we dislike at one point or another, so when these people arrive, it is important to take steps toward dealing with them responsibly. Some of the best things that you can do in these situations are to:

Show respect

You are never obligated to get along with everyone you work with, but you are, in many ways, obligated to show them all respect. When these situations arise, pride and ego are two things which you should set aside, even if the other party(s) are not willing to. This will allow you to come out of the experience with your dignity intact, whatever the outcomes may be.

Be assertive

If a coworker is rude or unprofessional to you, do not be afraid to tell them so. If you do so with certainty and fairness, they might be inclined to change some of their attitudes and behaviors in the future.

Anger/aggravation

Anger is arguably the most destructive emotion contained in a human. This is especially true when the anger is out of control in the workplace. It is also an emotion which most of us do not handle very well. As far as work is concerned, there is typically very little room for anger, which is problematic because much of it then gets taken home with us. Controlling this emotion is one of the most important steps in keeping any given job, especially for those who have difficulties with this. Some tips for dealing with this emotion are listed below:

Watch for the early signs of anger

No one else can detect when your anger is building up quite like you can, so detecting it early is your own responsibility. As was mentioned before, you decide how to react to situations, so if you react in anger, no one holds accountability for that happening.

When anger arises, take a break from what you are doing. When you start to get angry, closing your eyes and trying the aforementioned deep breathing exercises can help you hugely. These actions will do a lot to interrupt your angry thoughts and help to put your mind back on a more positive, relaxed pathway, reducing irrational statements and decisions made.

Picture yourself when you get angry

Imagining how you look and behave will usually give you some well-needed perspective on the situation at hand. For example, if you have the urge to shout at a coworker, think about what you would look like doing so: flustered, mean, and demanding. With that imagery in mind, it is easy to see that you would not be a good coworker in making that decision.

Disappointment/unhappiness

Disappointment and unhappiness are two of the more pullulated emotions in modern workplaces. These two are almost equal to anger in their unhealthiness; in fact, unhappiness may be unhealthier. These can also have detrimental impacts on your productivity, as they can leave you feeling exhausted and drained, and also less inclined to take risks in the future. Here are some steps that can be taken to curtail the effects of these awful emotions.

Consider your mindset

Try to always keep in mind that things will not always go your way. If they did, then life would become prosaic and meaningless. It is, sometimes, the adversity and the suffering that give life its meat. Do not try to avoid these things, the answer to these problems lies in the willingness to confront them.

Set and adjust your goals

Disappointment can often stem from neglecting to reach a goal. This rarely means, however, that the goal is no longer reachable. It is natural to feel disappointment in these situations, but you must always find the willpower to pick yourself back up. You could, for example, keep your goal, but just make a small change. Anything that will help you to get past the disappointments that you face.

Record your thoughts

One method for dealing with negative emotions is to write them down. When you feel unhappy or disappointed, try writing down what is bothering you, and be specific about your concerns. Is it your job that is bothering you? A coworker? Do you have too heavy of a workload? Writing these concerns down will help you to single out what exactly is bothering you and how you can improve on these areas of concern. Remember that you always have more powers than you think in improving a situation.

Remember to smile

Forcing a smile onto your face can actually make you feel happier and relieve stress. In addition, this activity also releases the neurotransmitters dopamine, endorphins, and serotonin, which all lower heart rate and blood pressure. The endorphins released also act as natural painkillers, and the serotonin acts as a natural antidepressant. Smiling will also make you look more attractive to those around you, further bettering the relationships you have with your coworkers.

Now that the main emotions that have adverse effects on most workers have been covered, let's take a look at some more strategies for dealing with these:

Compartmentalize your stressors

Try to keep stress and baggage from work and home in those respective places. You can use mental techniques, such as imagining the stressors locked away in a box for the time being. If you do not try to compartmentalize these issues, then waters will get very muddied up in your personal life, and things will become very complicated.

Identify your own self-talk

Relay to yourself what you tell yourself. By doing this, you may find yourself repeating thoughts and phrases to yourself that are not necessarily true or helpful. Try to identify your own thoughts that may be misleading or based on thinking errors. Doing this will help you move on from some of your worse points and attitudes into a more productive and expansive mindset.

Identify and accept your emotion

There is virtually nothing you can do to control an emotion that you are not even willing to come to terms with having. It is like denying the existence of a spider right in front of your eyes, the spider will just get bigger and bigger until it is all that you can see. In identifying what emotion(s) you are having and accepting that they are a natural part of life, you are taking lots of power away from them. In doing this, you are also becoming a greater solver of your own problems.

Affirm your rights

There are many places in life, work especially, where you are bound to feel like you have no rights and no control over what happens to you. By identifying your rights and your powers, you are giving yourself some perspective on the things that are in and out of your control. After taking some time to do this, you may find that you are much more powerful than you think you are. This will improve your mood and your self-confidence to affirm these rights that you have.

Communicate strategically

Anyone can drone on about the things that they do not like, but it takes skill and grit to actually get things done to fix all their problems. When you are trying to communicate with others, especially disagreements, it is always important to be precise in your language. This will allow you to communicate your qualms more effectively, and it will also decrease the chance of having misunderstandings and heated arguments. When trying to get a point across, try to come into the situation with some idea of what you want to get accomplished and your probability of having a productive conversation will increase dramatically. If others reply emotionally, let them vent and be understanding. You may learn more from them than they will from you. Ask for more details as well, and the two of you will probably come closer to an understanding because of it.

Be objective

Try to look at whatever is bothering you from both analytic and synthetic approaches. An analytic approach will help you understand the one issue with more depth and clarity, while a synthetic approach will help you understand the issue within the class of all of your possible issues. It is important to look into things with depth and focus, but seeing things as parts of your whole understanding will help you to make connections and find out why these certain things bother you through free associations.

Emotions are never right or wrong, they are only felt. There is no shame in feeling emotions unless of course, the emotion is shame. Emotions will always come and go and are always wiser than the ego. Each one of us, however, has free will in how we react to life's vicissitudes. Controlling emotions is not always easy; in fact, sometimes it becomes nearly impossible. But this skill is just like any other in that it can be improved with practice and diligence.

Chapter Three:

Building Confidence and Finding Long-Lasting Success

Low self-esteem is one of the most detrimental traits a person can have to overall well-being. One of the trickiest things about this trait is that it can be very deeply rooted in negative childhood experiences and then compounded by more negative experiences later in adulthood, such as ill-health, getting a divorce, losing a job, toxic relationships, or a general sense of having no control.

Low self-esteem can also increase the likelihood of developing mental health disorders and the severity of their effects. This trait has a complex and often comorbid relationship with disorders such as borderline personality disorder and depression. In depression, for instance, the disorder of depression can lead to a lowering of self-esteem, which in turn can lead to more depression. This is a destructive personality trait that can work with so many other factors to damage and destroy you.

Those who suffer from low self-esteem often view the world as a very hostile and unwelcoming place and themselves as its victim. This is not a great worldview to take, as people who see the world in this way are often reluctant to assert and express themselves. They then miss out on valuable opportunities and experiences that they otherwise would have had, feeling powerless to live life to its fullest. This creates yet another systemic loop of missing out on life, followed by feeling more and more inferior. It is easy to get caught up on this, but sometimes very hard to get out of it.

Here are some tips and techniques on how to build your confidence and avoid the systems of self-degradation that low self-esteem can cause:

Make two lists: one listing your achievements, and one listing your strengths

It may be beneficial to include a second party in this process, as low self-esteem can morph our self-perceptions to a point at which it becomes impossible to be objective when qualifying ourselves. Doing this will immediately make you feel more confident and ready to take on the day's challenges. It will also give you some perspective on where your personal development is at. This is a great means of boosting self-esteem and finding out what traits you possess that you can use to your advantage in the future.

Look at yourself in a more positive light

You have intrinsic value. You are a unique person, and there is something sovereign about you. You are the architect of your life, you build its foundations and choose its contents. It is important to remind yourself of these things throughout life. Looking at yourself through a positive light is the only way you can afford to look at yourself, and it makes life so much easier. When negative thoughts such as "I am a loser" or "no one wants me around" come to mind, it is your responsibility to identify and challenge those thoughts. Treat yourself like someone who deserves to be purged of thoughts like those, because they never help you.

Pay more attention to your personal hygiene

Take regular showers, brush your teeth, clip your nails and so on. Outside appearances are known to affect self-concept.

Wear only clean clothes that make you feel confident

Try wearing the clothes that you think you and the others around you will like the best. Consider throwing out some of your old, worn-out clothes for newer, better clothes.

Eat good foods as part of a healthier, more balanced diet

The benefits of doing this are innumerable. This tip should be followed above all others listed here. You should also make mealtime an especially mindful and relaxing time, taking time to enjoy every moment. This is also the time of the day when your senses are most active.

Exercise regularly

This is another incredibly important tip. Set some time away each day, say 20 to 30 minutes, for a brisk walk or a bike ride. In addition, it could help to set aside time 3 to 4 times a week for more vigorous forms of exercise. These could be weight lifting, team sports, martial arts, and so on. This will not only increase your self-esteem, but it will also reduce your risk of chronic disease, increase your energy levels, and even improve the functioning of your brain.

Get enough sleep at night

This is a big factor in living a healthy life that all too often gets ignored by modern people. Getting an appropriate amount of sleep each night (7 to 9 hours) can not only boost your mood and your self-esteem, but it can also reduce your risk of developing heart disease and/or high blood pressure. Doing this also makes your waking life more enjoyable and productive.

Reduce levels of stress

There are many different means of doing this. Deep breathing exercises, exercise, and venting to others come to mind. This will increase your confidence because, in part, of all the things that you will accomplish, you will increase your energy.

Make your living space clean, neat, comfortable, and attractive

Seeing clutter, dirt, and general disorganization activates the same neural pathways that seeing predators like snakes and spiders activates. You also feel about the same in the two instances, flustered and uncomfortable. This is why it is wise to keep your living space tidy, to clear up your mind if nothing else.

Do the things that you enjoy doing more often

This one may be obvious, but taking part in activities that you enjoy will make you much more fulfilled and confident. You can get all of your work done and fulfill all of your obligations in a day and still be able to do the things that you enjoy doing if you are persistent.

Pursue artistic endeavors

Painting, practicing an instrument, writing, dancing, whatever artistic activity you prefer will help to boost your confidence and happiness. It will also reduce your levels of stress. You might even find that you have artistic talents the likes of which you were not aware of. You never know until you try.

Set challenges for yourself that you can realistically meet

Setting goals that are out of your league can be a good way to boost productivity, but they also may reduce your self-esteem if you always expect to meet them. It is advisable to be realistic with yourself when setting your own personal goals. If you are, then you won't feel stretched thin, and you will be able to meet your own expectations more easily.

Get started on some of the things that you have been putting off

Finishing the tasks that you procrastinate on is always a great way to relieve stress and anxiety. It leaves you with free time afterward to relax and unwind. This will also boost your confidence by showing you your own competence and work ethic.

Be nice to people, and do things for them

Being altruistic will not only give you the immediate feeling of joy, but it will also make others appreciate you more, in turn making you even more confident. You will gain the respect of others as well as additional self-respect by behaving in this manner.

All these tips mentioned above should help to boost your self-esteem. This trait is, however, always going to be a work in progress for those of us who have low self-esteem. This is why it is important to stay persistent in fending off these sometimes die hard self-debasing traits and attitudes. Once some confidence has been found, however, it becomes beneficial to know what to do with it. How do you become successful with your new attitude, and how do you maintain that success? Hopefully, these next few tips will help you to answer those questions.

Aim big

This one is thrown around a lot but very rarely adhered to. Michelangelo, a centuries-old ideogram of success, once said that "the greater danger for most of us lies not in setting our aim too high and falling short, but in setting our aim too low, and achieving our mark." This quote holds especially true when imagining if Michelangelo had never become an artist, taking instead a "normal" day job. It is hard to tell where art would be today as a result.

Here we have the idea of hefty goals never being met as preferable to small goals successfully achieved. This is obviously not always the appropriate strategy in goal setting, but as we get older, we tend to lose energy and get a bit more lackluster in our goals and operations. Keeping your ambition is like keeping your youth, you get to retain so much of your potential and energy. So many people place realism over their aspirations, which is fine for them, but it should be noted that there is room for the both of them despite your age or walk in life.

Find what it is that you love to do most and do it

Media mogul Oprah Winfrey once said "you know you are on the road to success if you would do your job, and not be paid for it." This is a great one to consider while at work. If you can imagine yourself being as successful as possible at your current job, you can probably see yourself spending most of your time doing this. If this happens to be a job that you hate doing, then this would mean only spending all your time doing things that you do not enjoy. There is no sense in living like this, so why not instead spend most of your time doing something that you love to do?

If you take this step and success did not meet you, then you still spent all your time doing the things you love to do the most. You also probably learned a lot and developed lots of skills surrounding whatever these activities are. Many people do the things that they love to do most on the side for years, just for the sake of doing those things.

Learn how to balance life well

Phil Knight, the CEO of Nike Inc., once said "there is an immutable conflict at work in life and in business, a constant battle between peace and chaos. Neither can be mastered, but both can be influenced. How you go about that is the key to success." Those who strive greatly for success often make the mistake of placing the object of their success at the center of their lives. While it is important to work hard and to stay on top of your obligations, it is more important to lead an enjoyable life.

Workers tend to think that their job, whatever it may be, may lead them to success if they just work harder. They often work for long hours late into their evenings each day to make success happen. This is ill-advised, however, because whatever gains that come out of it come at the costs of their health, rest, and even their lives being enjoyable. This type of lifestyle burns people out and often makes them resentful as a result. To add to that, the successes that they do gain are usually only marginal. This lifestyle also destroys a worker's personal and social life. It leaves no time to go out with friends and little time to work on personal projects. Maintaining a balance between work and social life is one of the hallmarks of success that needs to be managed carefully and persistently.

Lose your fear of failure

Henry Ford, the founder of Ford motors, once said "failure is simply the opportunity to begin again, this time more intelligently." There is an anecdote of yet another important figure of the industrial revolution in respect to this tip; it took Thomas Edison several hundred failed attempts before he created the first successful light bulb. Afterward, one interviewer asked him "how do you feel after all of your failed attempts?" His response was tactful and wise: "I did not fail, I learned hundreds of ways *not* to invent the lightbulb."

From each and every one of his "failures," he took away a lesson of some sort. From these, he gained perspective on what would and would not work. He used a good attitude and an eye for finding helpful experiences to lead to his eventual success. This is the way that anyone who strives for success must conduct themselves.

The moral of the Thomas Edison story could be to monitor and learn from your own failures and turn them into valuable learning experiences. These will give you better ideas on how and how not to go about your work. You will also learn a lot about the work itself.

Keep your resolution to succeed unwaveringly

Colonel Sanders, the founder of KFC, was once quoted as saying "I made a resolve then that I was going to amount to something if I could. And no hours, nor amount of labor, nor the amount of money would deter me from giving the best that there was in me. And I have done that ever since, and I win by it. I know."

This tip is incredibly important, and it can be used in tandem with the one listed below very effectively. Giving up on your goals after a failure is the easiest thing in the world to do. If the failure is large and devastating enough, it can even seem like the only option. It takes, however, a burning and inextinguishable desire to succeed to curtail these defeatist urges though.

You have to put 100% into the things you go into, or else your plans will always fall through. If you do not give your goals everything that you have then each failure and each setback is going to hurt and dissuade you even more than the last. This will continue until you push back and fight for your dreams with everything that you have.

Success, in whatever form, is a hard thing to achieve. If it were easy to achieve, then everyone would be successful, but it instead discriminates against those who do not work for it. It is not possible to find success without grit and sacrifice, a point which brings us to our last tip on finding long-lasting success.

Be a person of action

Leonardo Da Vinci, one of the greatest geniuses of all time, once observed "it had long since come to my attention that people of accomplishment rarely sat back and let things happen to them. They went out and happened to things." This one will not only lead you to success, but it will also lead you to be mean and to be proud. The world is not kept running by people waiting for things to just happen to them, it is kept running by industrious people taking charge of themselves and the responsibilities they keep. It is useless to sit around and expect magic beans. It is almost always useful, however, to get to work on making your aspirations realities.

The tips and techniques mentioned above should help to bolster your self-esteem and make you more successful. If these goals are important to you, try applying these techniques in your everyday life and see if they work for you.

Chapter Four:

Social Engineering and Leadership

The importance of social engineering and leadership are often underestimated by contemporary thinkers. Most people are so absorbed in manipulating and taking down hierarchical structures that they neglect to figure out how to manifest themselves within these structures. Whether you have a proclivity toward leadership or not, it still remains important to have a working knowledge of leadership and how it works among groups of people.

Leaders, above all else, help themselves and others in making steps toward doing the right things. In doing this, they build an inspiring vision, set direction, and create new possibilities. Leadership is, in part, about mapping out the route to your team's successful future. It is challenging, but also exciting, dynamic, and inspiring. Setting the direction of the pack is not the only responsibility of a leader though. They are also obligated to guide their people in these directions in a smooth and efficient way. This may be the more challenging skill which takes more time to develop.

This chapter and its tips on the process of leadership will be based on the "transformational model" of leadership proposed by James MacGregor Burns and further developed by Bernard Bass. This model more so focuses on bringing about change through visionary leadership than the normative managerial processes designed to maintain the current performance of given groups.

An overview of leadership

The following are a few traits of an effective leader:

1. Succeeds in creating an inspiring vision of the future
2. Inspires and motivates people to engage with that vision
3. Manages the delivery of the vision
4. Builds and coaches a team, so that it becomes more effective in meeting the vision

Effective leadership requires all of these traits working together with one another. Next, it would be helpful to explore each one of these elements in greater detail.

Succeeds in creating an inspiring vision of the future

In the workforce, a vision that a boss prognosticates needs to be a convincing, realistic, and attractive depiction of the situation that you want to be in in the future. This vision should set priorities, and provide direction and a marker to people to assure that all are able to see whether or not the goals set forth have been achieved.

To create a reliable vision, leaders must first assess and analyze their current situation to get an understanding of where to go. Some steps that are appropriate to take in this stage are considering the evolution of their industry in the future, considering the behaviors of their competitors, and how to innovate successfully to shape their business for competition in the future marketplace. The next step is to undergo some scenario analysis to assess the validity of their vision.

Leadership is, therefore, proactive rather than reactive; looking ahead, problem-solving, and constantly evolving.

Once a leader's vision has been developed, it is necessary to sell the vision. To do this, they have to make the vision compelling and convincing. A compelling vision allows people to understand, embrace, see, and feel it. Effective leaders can communicate their visions effectively and clearly. They are able to speak about their visions in ways that people can relate to, and they inform people in an inspired way. This makes people more receptive to their ideas and more inclined to follow what they have to say.

Shared values and vision creation are two major components of leadership. Those who can develop skills in these two areas are more likely to succeed in leadership roles.

Inspires and motivates people to engage with that vision

The foundation of leadership is a compelling vision. This vision is only met, however, by a leader's ability to inspire and motivate their followers. At the beginning of most projects, it is easier to stay enthusiastic, which in turn makes it easier to win support for it than in other stages of the project. Afterward, the initial enthusiasm fades is when it becomes more difficult to maintain an inspiring vision moving forward. People change along with their attitudes and working methods, as well as their goals. Good leadership requires recognizing this phenomenon and working hard throughout a given project to be cognizant of others' needs, hopes, and desires while meeting the vision at hand. It is a juggling act of altruism and pragmatism that helps wherever it goes.

One means of linking effort, motivation, and outcome is known as expectancy theory. This place is an emphasis on leaders linking two main expectations that their followers have. These are listed below:

- The expectation of hard work leading to good results.
- The expectation of good results leading to incentives or rewards.

People with these expectations foresee both intrinsic and extrinsic rewards and therefore work harder to achieve success.

One other approach includes repeatedly restating the vision with added emphasis on its rewards and communicating the vision in a more effective and attractive way.

Expert power is one of the most helpful things that a leader can have. People are more inclined to admire and believe in leaders with this because they are seen as experts at what they do. Expertise comes with credibility, respect, and prestige. This also potentially gives people a right and even an obligation to lead others. Having and displaying competence gives leaders a much easier time motivating and inspiring their followers.

Natural charisma and appeal can also serve as conduits for a leader's motivation of and influence over people, as well as other sources of power. These other sources of power include the ability to assign tasks to people and to pay bonuses.

Managing the delivery of the vision

This area of leadership applies more to management than any of these other tips.

Leaders always need to make sure that they are properly managing the work necessary for delivering their vision. This can be done by either themselves, a manager, or a team of managers delegated by the leader to deliver the vision of the leader.

To achieve this, team members need to meet their performance goals linked to the company's vision.

Some means of seeing that this is done are KPIs (key performance indicators), performance management, and project management. One other way of ensuring that the vision is being met is a management style called management by wandering around (MBWA). This style ensures that all the steps that need to be taken are taken in meeting any given goals.

Another trait of an effective leader is the ability to manage change well. Leadership is, after all, constant evolution and adjusting to work's vicissitudes. Managing changes smoothly and efficiently ensures that all goals will be met and obstacles overcome throughout the course of realizing the leader's vision. This can only be done, however, with the backing and support of the people behind the leader.

Building and coaching a team to achieve the vision

Some of the more crucial activities carried out by transformational leaders are individual and team development. Without these, there would be nothing for the leader to lead. The first step in developing a team that a leader has to take is to come to understand team dynamics. There are several popular and well-established models that can describe these to a leader, including Belbin's team roles approach, and the forming, storming, norming, performing, and adjourning theory of Bruce Tuckman. A more in-depth analysis of this theory is featured below.

Forming

The forming step involves a team coming together at the beginning of a venture to figure out the goals of the group out and how to go about accomplishing these. Members tend to be impersonal and polite during this period as everyone is still getting oriented within the team.

Storming

The storming phase is a bit more selective and critical. In this phase, the leadership may be questioned along with group members ideas. This is very much a culling-off phase of the process as many of the group's members will feel overwhelmed and disconcerted by the turbulence and criticism. Some of them who do not leave after this stage give up on the goal at hand as well. And some just simply do not want to do what is asked of them.

Norming

Norming is the step at which the group comes together to agree on a singular plan for achieving the common goal. In this stage, members of the group are encouraged to yield their ideas for the betterment of the group, and they also come to know and understand each other better, building stronger relationships. It is the working toward a common goal that brings the team members together.

Performing

By the performing stage of the process, the group members are able to work toward accomplishing the goal without very much outside supervision or input. They also come to understand each other's needs better and how to work with one another to accomplish the goal at hand.

Adjourning

In the adjourning stage, the opportunity to reflect on unsuccessful and successful outcomes comes about. Members of the group can use these outcomes to gauge what they should do when working on future tasks. This will help smooth out the process of meeting a goal in the future.

The next time you find yourself working in a group on a certain task, monitor the group's progress through these stages. Group members tend to move through these stages in all sorts of different orders. They actually rarely happen in the order listed above. If, however, team members are aware of the steps that they are moving through—which they usually are not—then they can typically work through these steps much more efficiently and effectively. Walking yourself through these steps listed above will help you navigate the happenings of your workplace better in the future.

Leadership

A competent leader always does their best to ensure that team members are equipped with all the abilities and skills necessary to do their jobs and achieve the overarching vision. To do this, it is necessary to give and receive feedback on a day-to-day basis, as well as to train and coach team members on a regular basis as well. These steps will improve individual and team performances dramatically.

Good leaders lead, but great leaders lead and find leadership potential. When leading a team, it is always helpful to find leadership abilities in others, whatever their current positions may be. This paves the way for not only differentiation in hierarchical status, but also for further development beyond the leader's influence or even stay. It can also give a leader a surprisingly helpful example in other competent workers.

The terms "leader" and "leadership" are often misused to describe people who are actually in managerial positions. These people are often highly skilled and have great work-ethics, but that does not necessarily make them great leaders.

Workplaces are all too often hoisted up on people who others consider to be leaders but are actually managers. These managers often do not provide any aspirations or even long-term goals for their team members, which is fine in the short term, but eventually leads to feelings of meaninglessness and even resentment.

The next discussion points that should be delved into would have to be group dynamics and social engineering. These are important realms to know about when entering a new workplace, or any given social setting for that matter. Here we will look into what group dynamics are and what you need to know about them to master them.

Group dynamics

Group dynamics, whether ignored by participants or not, play a major role in any culture, organization, or unit. People with differing ideas and perspectives make these groups up. It is very rare that all people and their ideologies are homogeneous within any given group. It is, in fact, also dangerous. Leaders are looked up to within these groups maintain the unity of purpose and cohesiveness of the unit. The cultural bonds within these units must be developed more at certain times than in others. Once these bonds are developed, the further effort has to be put in to nurture them.

Dysfunction within these groups occurs with alienation among specific members. When a member feels ostracized, there is very little keeping them from acting out in unpredictable ways. This is bound to come up at times and when it does, the leader can struggle to remain objective as the structure of the cohesive unit starts to fall apart. These are usually the worst periods of chaos in the histories of groups. It is these periods, however, that separate good leaders from bad ones.

At all times, if they are understandable or appropriate, the leader or manager must continue to recognize the team member causing the disturbance as an integral part of the group. Further alienation typically leads only to further disturbance. At these times, it would be beneficial for the leader to look at the employee causing the disturbance as being a special employee, one who could use the leader's help or skills, one who remains part of the group, and even one who may be there to teach the leader something. A review of the nature of the communication, power, and corporate climate of the unit would also be beneficial under these circumstances to further understand the team member's point of view and avoid further disturbances in the future.

A leader must also have abilities in objective introspection. It is not advisable or even possible to guide or help others unless these skills are developed. It is putting the cart before the horse. A leader recognizing their own insecurities will be more easily able to perceive and recognize staff dysfunctions as being symptomatic of systematic dysfunctions. The ego will be more open to rationality once personal problems are more specifically addressed. It takes a secure and mature person to decide that their staff is ultimately more important than their own ideas, moving forward.

Once new steps are taken after dysfunctions, much progress can be made, and the company can often be left better off than they were beforehand because of this. The staff can find new means of communication and ways to relate to one another, they can find also find new modes of behavior all together that could even boost their self-esteem or overall well-being. Fortunately, for the leader, everyone at the company could then boast of having a manager with a plethora of newfound ideas and attitudes. All these intricacies and regulations tend to make working in a group very complicated at times, but if all of these steps are stuck to, and everyone pulls their own weight, the benefits of teamwork can be innumerable.

Conclusion

Thank you for making it through to the end of *Emotional Intelligence*. Let's hope it was informative and answered any questions you had previously regarding the subject. The purpose of this book was primarily to supply you with some tools for fostering your emotional intelligence. This is, however, a trait that takes lots of time and effort to improve on. The next steps for you would be to consider looking into any other resources on this subject and seeing if any are a good fit for you.

This book's subject was broad. Emotional intelligence is a wide concept with lots of components, which means that there is a lot of room for improvement. This book mostly covered emotional intelligence through a lens suitable for use in the workplace, but to truly gain skills in dealing with your emotions you have to live a lifestyle, of sorts, devoted to that goal, in and outside of work.

The workplace is a very important place to keep your emotions under control though. Attitudes and demeanors that are acceptable in most of the public arena just aren't in many workplaces. It is always ideal to separate your work life from your home life, of course, but it is even more ideal to keep a demeanor that is acceptable and respectable everywhere you go.

Finally, thank you again for finishing this book. Continue to apply the principles mentioned here in your life, and you are bound to see some positive changes.

www.ingramcontent.com/pod-product-compliance
Ingram Content Group UK Ltd.
Pitfield, Milton Keynes, MK11 3LW, UK
UKHW022155230426
12049UKWH00022BA/181/J